BRITNEY SPEARS

TRIUMPH
ENTERTAINMENT
Division of Triumph Books
601 South LaSalle Street
Chicago, Illinois 60605

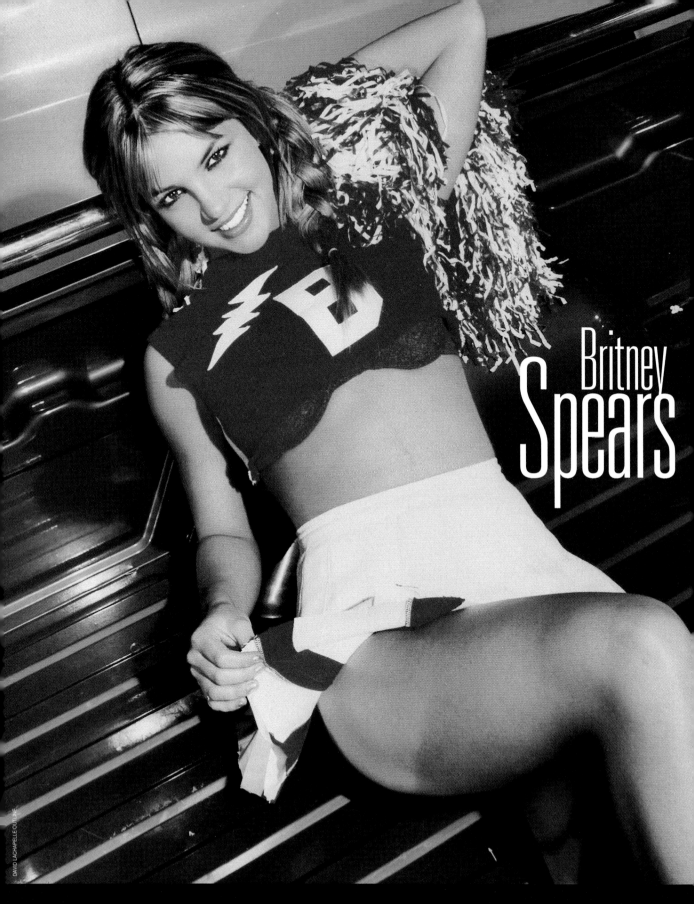

Britney
Spears

CONTENTS

She's all That

Britney Spears basks in the **pop** music spotlight, but still **manages** to stay **down** to earth

By George Gardner

a

WORLD-FAMOUS MOUSE GAVE BRITNEY JEAN SPEARS HER SHOT AT STARDOM. Now she's all grown up and wants to reach the top of the charts one more time.

With the May 16 release of her new album, "Oops! ... I Did It Again!" Britney is eager to prove she's no mere flash in the pan. (As if we ever doubted it!) Currently in rehearsals for her U.S. tour that begins June 16, this southern belle-turned-international superstar has never been content to wait for success to fall into her lap. She's a seize-the-day kind of chick who knows what she wants and how to get it, even when the cards seem to be stacked against her.

For those of you who aren't already familiar with Britney's Cinderella story, here's what you need to know: Like most girls in America, Britney grew up singing into her hairbrush, wondering what it would be like to take center stage at concerts packed with screaming fans. While it's just a fairy tale for most people, Britney was determined not to live her life asking, "What if?"

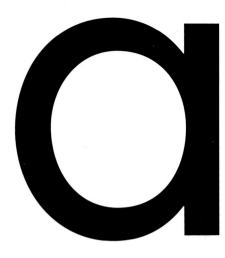

MARC BAPTISTE/OUTLINE (4)

Despite her natural ability and ambition, Britney's success was not simply handed to her. Take her first audition for "The New Mickey Mouse Club," for example. After persuading her mom to let her try out for a spot on the program, Britney was rejected by producers, who told her she was too young. Still, even this bad news had a silver lining: A producer from the show sensed that young Britney had what it takes to be a star someday, and he offered to hook her up with a talent agent in New York City.

Paying with Sweat

For the next few years, fame took a back seat as Britney paid her dues and struggled to prove her worth. She took dance classes and attended a performing arts school in Manhattan, hoping to find some way to stand out among all the other talented teenagers. Eventually, her hard work paid off and she landed a few commercials, a role in an off-Broadway play and a chance to compete on the television talent show "Star Search." Although life in the big city was a tough transition for the little Louisiana sweetheart, she vowed not to give up.

"I guess it's just the way I was brought up," said Britney. "My mom always said, 'Go for what you want.'"

When the opportunity arose to audition again for "The New Mickey Mouse Club," Britney had grown in age and experience. This time, the producers loved what they saw. At age 11, she was the ➔

With the release of
her new album,
Britney says, "I'm
more confident, and
I think that shows in
the material."

BRITNEY 7

Britney had been considered for an all-girl group called Innosense, but a successful solo career beckoned instead.

youngest Mouseketeer to join the show. Fellow castmates included Keri Russell of "Felicity" and *NSync members JC Chasez and Justin Timberlake.

"It was like a dream come true," said Britney. "It was all I really wanted, and when they called on the phone and said, 'You're going to be a Mouseketeer,' I just started screaming."

Back to Square One

Although life on the fun-filled show in Orlando was exciting for Britney, she had to face a harsh reality when the show was canceled in 1994. The very disappointed youngster returned to Louisiana and tried to readjust to a "normal" life. Imagine how hard it must have been for her to enroll in high school and be a regular kid when all she really wanted to do was perform!

Britney soon fell into the routines of an average teenager, but she was still restless and dreamed about a return to the spotlight.

"I can't say I missed out on my teenage years," she said. "I got to go out with friends and go to dances. It was wonderful, but then I got really bored."

Britney would occasionally travel to New York for auditions, eager for another shot at stardom.

"I'm always wanting to get up and go," she told a Louisiana newspaper reporter at the time. "Lots of times, I'll be home and just sitting there watching TV, and I'll be wishing I was on an airplane to New York or Los Angeles or Florida."

Britney landed an audition for a new girl band called Innosense. She sang her heart out for the tryout and, of course, she blew the competition away. Once again, however, she was rejected. This time it wasn't her age that hindered her – it was immense talent! The band's manager

"I have **really strong morals,** and just because **I look** sexy on the cover of **Rolling Stone** doesn't mean I'm a **naughty girl.** I thought the pictures were **fine."**

actually claimed she was too good to join the group! He advised Britney to pursue a solo career and sent her demo tape to Jive Records. The record label saw Britney's star potential and immediately offered her a development deal, which led to a solo recording contract that would go on to make history.

The Album Takes Shape

Working with several well-known writers and music producers, including veteran Backstreet Boys collaborators Max Martin and Denniz Pop, Britney's debut album came together quickly in the spring of 1998. Although her original vision had been for a more adult contemporary sound, the singer soon realized that she was perfectly suited to sing more danceable pop tunes. Britney spent several months in Stockholm, Sweden, recording the songs for an album that would eventually spawn four Top 40 singles.

Later that summer, Britney started a promotional tour to showcase songs on the debut album. Although she was still relatively unknown, Britney performed her heart out at shopping malls across the country and visited radio stations for in-studio interviews.

On November 3, 1998, Britney's first single, "...Baby One More Time," was released, and the fan reaction was enormous. One week after the release of her album of the same name on January 13, 1999, Britney received a wake-up call from the president of her record company, Jive, who told her the album and the single had reached the top of the Billboard charts simultaneously. It was official: Britney was the new princess of pop, the hottest female teen to rock pop's boy-dominated world. ➔

"Of course, I had hopes and dreams of this. But no, I didn't really expect all this to happen," Britney told reporters. "But it feels good."

On The Road

The next thing the young singer knew, she was the opening act for *NSync, which was touring small theaters in support of its multiplatinum debut album in late 1998 and early 1999. Although Britney's first single had already received radio airplay, many *NSync fans remained unfamiliar with her. Warming up a crowd that had not yet warmed up to her was a little frightening, and she feared she would be booed off the stage.

"The fans didn't know me," said Britney. "I was like, 'I'm really young! Please don't be mean to me!'"

You'd think touring the country would have been enough to keep the bright-eyed beauty very busy, but she had much more business to tend to. Britney knew she would have to come up with a great video for the increasingly popular single "...Baby One More Time." Jive Records representatives wanted the video to feature a Power Rangers-type scenario with Britney as a superhero, but Britney thought the idea was too childish and had the courage to explain her own vision to record execs.

"I was freaking out because they were really set on the idea," Britney told US magazine. "So I told them my idea instead."

Britney wanted the "...Baby One More Time" video to be set inside a high school and feature a lot of dancing, and she ended up selling Jive Records on the concept. Britney said the whole video-making process made her aware of her celebrity status for the first time.

"It really hit me when I did the video for '...Baby,'" said Britney. "I was like, 'Oh my God, all of these people are working for me!'"

Something To Talk About

Until this time, Britney had still been pegged as just an adorable, angel-eyed former Mouseketeer. But once people caught a glimpse of Britney in her sizzling new video, their perceptions started to change. In fact, some controversy surrounded the "sexiness" of Britney's video attire: a super-mini schoolgirl uniform and shirt that exposed much of her midriff.

" I can't say I missed out on my **teenage** years. I got to go out **with friends** and go to dances. It was **wonderful,** but then **I got really** bored. "

Britney scoffed at the criticism in an interview with *Rolling Stone.*

"All I did was tie up my shirt!" she said. "And a lot of people my age wear thigh-highs."

Of course, the *Rolling Stone* interview only added fuel to the fire, since the pop diva graced that issue's cover wearing what many considered to be inappropriate attire for a girl her age.

The singer later commented on her decision to make waves.

"What's the big deal?" she said. "I have really strong morals, and just because I look sexy on the cover of *Rolling Stone* doesn't mean I'm a naughty girl. I thought the pictures were fine."

Britney also had to laugh at the fact that the lyrics of her hit single, ("Hit me, baby, one more time") were thought to condone violence.

"It doesn't mean physically hit me!" she said emphatically. "I think it's kind of funny that people would actually think that's what it meant."

Following the mind-boggling success of her album's debut, Britney began touring again in early 1999, but was sidelined by a knee injury she sustained during a dance practice. The injury and subsequent surgery forced Britney to stay home and recuperate. She admits the mishap was probably a good thing because it gave her some much-needed time to rest.

When she finally recovered, Britney was ready to hit the road once again, but this time she wouldn't be the opening act – she would be the headliner. Sponsored by Tommy Jeans, Britney's "...Baby One More Time" tour landed her in more than 50 cities throughout the United States and Canada. Diverse artists such as Michael Fredo, C-Note, Steps and Boyz-N-Girlz United warmed up crowds before Britney's glitzy performance. Among the tour's highlights was a section honoring music legends during which Britney performed tunes by Madonna and Janet Jackson as well as the Journey ballad "Open Arms."

Once and Again

After the summer tour, Britney did everything but slow down. In addition to working on "Oops! ... I Did It Again!" she planned to co-author a book with her mother, Lynn (it's due in stores this summer) and consider acting offers. While a guest stint on the WB teen drama "Dawson's Creek" did not pan out, Britney is undaunted. ➜

Britney looks radiant
and glamorous at the
American Music
Awards in January.

Britney 411

Full Name: Britney Jean Spears **Hometown:** Kentwood, La.

Birthdate: December 2, 1981 **Zodiac Sign:** Sagittarius

Height: 5 feet 5 inches **Weight:** 130 pounds

Hair Color: Blonde **Eye Color:** Brown

"This **is** the life **I** have always wanted to have."

"There have been some scripts that are really, really good," she said. "It's really just a matter of finding the time to fit it into the schedule."

Britney also assembled a second leg to the "...Baby One More Time" tour, hitting major U.S. arenas through April 2000. While the show was very similar to the one she performed the previous summer, it dropped the cover tunes in favor of two songs from her new album. For the first song, a ballad called "Don't Let Me Be The Last To Know," Britney's fantastic dancers took a break and Britney soared over – and tantalizingly close to – the crowd on a huge "magic carpet." The second song was the title track to the new album, a Janet Jackson-style jam that Britney says will be her next single.

With her sophomore album scheduled for release on May 16, the pop diva's life won't be slowing down any time soon. Britney describes the sound of the album as being a little bit funkier and having a more mature sound.

"This album is definitely more mature than the first one," Britney told MTV Radio Network. "I had more input, and I was a lot more confident in the studio. You'll be able to hear that when you listen to the album. I can't wait to go on tour and perform the new songs. It's gonna be hot!"

Britney has also added songwriter to her long list of credentials. She co-wrote one of the songs on the new album, "Dear Diary," which she describes as a tribute to a girl's innermost thoughts.

Britney told a New Orleans newspaper in April that her expectations for her new album are realistic; she knows the phenomenal sales of her debut likely won't be repeated.

"I don't think you ever really expect anything," she said. "I was very curious and very hopeful and I wanted the (first) album to do really well, because I had worked for a really long time. And then when it took off, I was really, really excited. And with this next album I can just, you know, just pray about it and hope that it will do the same, but it's kind of hard to follow up '...Baby One More Time,' which has sold like 17 million worldwide.

"But I know this material is better," continued Britney. "It's just something that kind of changed by itself, and with me being older my voice has changed a little bit and I'm more confident, and I think that shows in the material."

Staying Busy

The coming year will undoubtedly be packed with more celebrity appearances, stadium-filled concerts and, she hopes, many more awards shows. It's a lot to ask of an 18-year-old young woman, but Britney makes the best of it.

"I don't live a completely normal life because I'm not a typical teenager who goes to school every day," she said. "But I try to make my life as normal as possible."

With this much success under her belt, Britney doesn't have to worry about turning back into a normal teenager at the stroke of midnight. Her debut album has sold 11 million copies and counting, and she earned a cool $15 million in 1999.

Still, the singer never forgets where she came from. Her mom doesn't let her forget it either. After all, she still has to do chores around the house, just like the rest of us.

"I wash the dishes, I vacuum, I clean, I make the bed," said Britney. "I do everything!" ❤

Fifty Britne

Think you know all there is
to know about Miss Spears?
See how many of these Fun
Facts you already knew!

By Amy Helmes

yFunFacts

1. RAGIN' CAJUN
Britney was a bayou baby.
Her hometown is Kentwood, La.
(population: 1,200), about an
hour's drive north of New Orleans.

FiftyBritneyFunFacts

2. PUPPY LOVE
For Christmas, Britney's mom gave her a Yorkie teacup puppy named Mitzi. After some extensive potty training, Mitzi can now accompany Britney on tour.

3. RAISING THE ROOF
She and her mother, Lynne, are designing an English Tudor-style dream house.

4. ROAD WARRIOR
Britney loves riding four-wheelers and go-carts with her sister, Jamie Lynn.

5. KNEE-SLAPPERS
Besides keeping her safe, Britney's bodyguards provide an extra service — making her laugh.

6. COLLECT CALL
When she's on tour, Britney calls her mom nearly every night.

7. ROOM WITH A VIEW ... OF THE FREEWAY!
Brit's room on her tour bus is painted lilac and decorated with gifts from fans.

8. THE WEDDING SINGER
Before she made it big, Britney performed at relatives' weddings.

9. FAN MAIL
Candles and dolls are a few of the favorite gifts Britney has received from fans.

10. GLASS SLIPPERS
Britney collects tiny porcelain shoes.

11. NICE NIGHT OUT
The pop star's idea of a perfect date is a good movie and a nice meal at a restaurant.

12. GLOBE-TROTTING
Britney's favorite vacation spots are jolly old England and the beautiful Bahamas.

13. COLLEGE PREP
Britney says she'd eventually love to go to college and study entertainment law.

14. SUN GODDESS
A favorite pastime is soaking up rays to perfect her tan. She'll even go to a tanning salon on cold or cloudy days.

15. GRAB THE KLEENEX!
Her favorite flicks: "Steel Magnolias" and "My Best Friend's Wedding."

16. HOT WHEELS
Britney recently purchased a convertible Jaguar but she can't find time to drive it!

17. PAGE TURNER
Trashy romance novels are Britney's guilty pleasure. Her favorite book is Danielle Steele's "Dangerous."

18. MOBILE MASTERPIECE
Britney thinks the cell phone is one of society's greatest inventions. She's always using hers to catch up with friends from home. She loves e-mail, too.

19. MAKING THE GRADE
Although she's a teen queen, Britney still has schoolwork. Her least favorite subjects? Geometry and Spanish.

20. MAGIC KINGDOM
As a former Mouseketeer, Britney knows her way around Walt Disney World. Her favorite attractions at the enormous theme park are Space Mountain and Rockin' Rollercoaster.

21. HOOP DREAMS
Britney has always felt at home on a basketball court, and she's a big fan of the Chicago Bulls.

22. BORN TO HAND JIVE
Britney is "hopelessly devoted" to the "Grease" movie soundtrack.

23. BIGGEST SLIP-UP
Even Britney has had a few embarrassing moments. Once, at an *NSync concert, she slipped on a cupcake and fell.

24. BEAUTY BUZZ
Her favorite brand of makeup is MAC.

25. THE NAME GAME
If Britney could choose a different name, she'd pick Madison or Alana.

26. QUIET RIOT
She may shine on stage, but in real life, Britney describes herself as quiet and shy.

27. SISTER ACT
Britney's most memorable moment was the birth of her little sister, Jamie Lynn.

28. MEAL TICKET
Chicken and dumplings and cookie dough ice cream are some of Britney's favorite foods.

29. DUELING DIVAS
Someday Britney would love to sing a duet with Madonna.

30. CHURCH LADY
Apparently, Britney is so religious that she's a little upset about having to miss church services while she's touring.

31. TWIST OF FATE
The man who wrote "...Baby One More Time" originally intended it to be sung by TLC, but he later changed his mind and gave it to Britney instead.

32. COOL THREADS
Although Britney has a personal stylist for most of her public appearances, some of her favorite designers include Betsey Johnson, bebe and Giorgio Armani.

33. I THEE WED?
Britney says she doesn't think she'll get married until she's at least 26 years old.

34. THIS LITTLE PIGGY...
Though Britney's feet are great for dancing, she likes that body part least.

35. CAFFEINE CONFUSION
Two of Britney's favorite drinks are Sprite and cappuccino.

36. CREATIVE LICENSE
The schoolgirl theme in the video for the No. 1 single "...Baby One More Time" was Britney's idea. It was reportedly the most requested video ever on MTV's "Total Request Live."

37. KISS AND TELL
Rumor has it Britney's first kiss was with *NSync's Justin Timberlake. They "went out" briefly while starring together on "The New Mickey Mouse Club."

38. SCARY MOMENT
A crazed fan once climbed into Britney's parents' bedroom window. Creepy!

39. OFF HER CHEST
Contrary to rumors, Britney swears that she has never gotten breast implants. She says anyone who believes that gossip is an "ignorant goofball."

40. SHATTERING RECORDS
Britney was the first female artist to simultaneously have the No. 1 pop single and No. 1 album (according to Billboard) in the United States.

41. TONGUE-TIED
Although Britney is a superstar in her own right, she says she gets nervous meeting other celebrities.

42. MAMA'S GIRL
Teenage girls may butt heads with their mothers, but Britney's is her best friend. She showed her gratitude by giving mom a new car and a diamond bracelet.

43. GAL PALS
Britney looks for complete honesty in a friend, even if she doesn't want to hear it. One good friend is Danielle Fishel, star of ABC's "Boy Meets World."

44. BREAK A LEG
Last year, Britney underwent knee surgery after she tore some cartilage during dance practice.

45. DID YOU KNOW?
The video for "...Baby One More Time" was shot at the same high school where the movie "Grease" was filmed.

46. METAL MOUTH
Her pearly whites may look perfect now, but it took a little work. Britney wore braces in high school.

47. BALANCING ACT
Britney was once enrolled in a gymnastics camp with legendary Olympic gymnastics coach Bela Karolyi. She kept a balance beam in her parents' living room.

48. COUCH POTATO
Britney's favorite TV shows are WB hits "Felicity" and "Dawson's Creek."

49. WHO'S THAT GIRL?
The woman who plays the teacher in the "...Baby One More Time" video is a close family friend who acts as Britney's guardian on the road.

50. CELEBRITY CRUSH
Like most teenage girls, Britney thinks Ben Affleck is a big-time hottie. (Unlike most girls, though, she got to have lunch with Ben!) She also digs Tom Cruise, Mel Gibson and Brad Pitt. ❤

Pinups!
Britney Spears

Britney Spears

HOOLS

Britney
Spears

Britney
Spears

Britney
Spears

Britney
Spears

Britney Spears

Britney
Spears

UP FRONT WITH BRITNEY

From rumors to realities, clothing to career, Miss Spears comes clean

By Nicole Neville

Gold Collectors Series: You're one of the busiest people in music – your life must be crazy! How do you take your mind off everything?

Britney: I just do normal things like call my mom and my girlfriends, or I go to the movies or the beach. I usually have one day off per week when I can sleep late and just hang out.

GCS: When you go home, do your old friends ever say they think you've changed since you've become famous?

B: No, not at all. We never feel weird; we're like sisters. If they kissed my butt, I would kick their butts!

GCS: Who are your closest friends?

B: I'm good friends with my dancers and my cousins from home; I've been friends with them my whole life. My mom's sister's daughter, Laura Lynne, we're very close. She's my age and our mannerisms are exactly alike.

GCS: Do you have new friends now that you're a star?

B: It's really hard to find friends. I am fortunate that the people who travel with me, especially my dancers, are really good friends. It works out very well.

GCS: What was your life like before you made it big?

B: Well, I was performing at malls. There was a little fashion show before I performed, and it was before my first single ("...Baby One More Time") came out, so no one really knew who I was. But it was cool because I had two dancers with me and we put on a cute little show. Everyone was really into it, and that made me feel good.➜

" **My mom is so positive about life. She's not negative; she always looks on the bright side of everything.** "

Britney with mom Lynne at the 1999 Teen Choice Awards

GCS: How did you first get into singing and dancing?

B: When I was little, we had a gym right beside our house, and there was this lady who taught dance there. I started dancing when I was really young. Then I started gymnastics. I'd sing to the radio all the time, and I was in the church choir, and I just realized that I loved to sing. I started doing competitions and I continued dancing, so it all kind of came together.

GCS: You starred on "The New Mickey Mouse Club" along with JC Chasez and Justin Timberlake of *NSync, not to mention Christina Aguilera. Everyone's really successful now. Did you keep in touch over the years?

B: I was going to be in a girl's group called Innosense before I got signed a solo deal with Jive Records. Justin's mom (who manages Innosense) and my mom kept in touch, and Lynn, Justin's mom, told me about it. But I signed with Jive instead, so I didn't join the group.

GCS: Do you have a role model?

B: Definitely my mom because she is so positive about life. She's not negative; she always looks on the bright side of everything. I really admire that. I would also love to meet Oprah Winfrey or Whitney Houston.

GCS: Is Madonna one of your heroes?

B: I just admire how she is able to reinvent herself and keep the public interested in her music.

GCS: We heard that Barbra Streisand is also a major influence.

B: Yeah. When I was younger, I listened to her music a lot, and I still listen to her periodically. I would love to meet her.

GCS: What do you think about little girls who want to be like you?

B: I think it is very flattering. I have a little sister, and it is really special to have her look up to me that way. She goes in my room and plays my music. She's so sweet. And she is so outspoken. She's totally different from what I was like when I was little. I was a very quiet child.

GCS: So do you think of yourself as a role model for other girls?

B: I think it's inevitable. When you're on ➜

Britney belts out one of her hits at the annual "Wango Tango" concert at Dodger Stadium in Los Angeles.

TV all the time and in magazines, you can't help but be one.

GCS: Is that a role you're willing to take on?
B: Yeah, definitely. It's really flattering that so many kids listen to my music. It's really cool!

GCS: So what's next besides singing? Producing? Acting?
B: I would love to act AND write songs. When I get time, I would love to act more.

GCS: Do you have any offers?
B: Oh yeah. I have some offers to be in some movies, and some of them are kind of, you know, so-so. Some scripts, though, have been really good, and I say, "I want to do that." It's just (a matter of) finding the time to fit filming a movie into my schedule.

GCS: You've already appeared on "Sabrina, the Teenage Witch," and you'll be in the upcoming movie "Jack of All Trades." Will there be more Britney on the big screen?
B: All I can say is I would definitely like to keep acting.

GCS: What's the deal with your movie role in "Jack of All Trades"?
B: I play a flight attendant. It's a small role.

GCS: You have said that you eventually want to go to college. Is that still true?
B: It is definitely something I want to do if I have time. To have that education would be wonderful. But what I really want to do with my life is to sing. So why should I go to college to learn to be, say, a lawyer, when I'm happy doing what I'm doing now?

GCS: Do you consider yourself to be a spiritual person?
B: I try to go to church whenever I can. I also have a prayer book that I write in every night. When I'm on the road I get so tired, and I used to find myself falling asleep when I'd say my prayers at night. So now I write my prayers down before I go to bed.

Fashion, Fun and Food

GCS: What kinds of clothes do you like to wear?
B: When I'm traveling, I'm typically tired, so that usually means I'm in sweats. When I go out to eat or go to parties, I usually wear (clothes from) bebe. My favorite store in the world is Abercrombie & Fitch. It's the best store because its clothes are all about comfort; it's cool and I love it.

GCS: Has fame changed the way you dress?
B: It hasn't really changed my style at all. I've always been a big sweats person, and I like putting my hair in a ponytail.

GCS: What do you have way too many of?
B: Probably sunglasses. Wherever I go – gas stations, Sunglass Hut – I'm always buying new shades!

GCS: How many pairs do you have?
B: I travel with about six pairs, but I have at least three dozen.

GCS: If you could change something about your appearance, what would it be?
B: I wish my hair was thicker, and I wish my feet were prettier. I don't like my feet. My toes – they're really ugly. I also wish my ears were smaller, and my nose could be smaller, too. I could go on and on (laughing)!

GCS: Have your eating habits changed since you became famous?
B: When I'm on the road, I tend to eat bad things – I can't help it. Like when I'm overseas, I typically don't want to eat all that weird stuff. I just want McDonald's to fill up my stomach. I normally eat whatever I want, but I'm trying to be a little bit healthier. When I go home to Louisiana, my mom cooks for me, so that's when I have my best meals! ➜

"I would love to act and write songs. When I get time, I would love to act more."

> **" I try to go to church whenever I can. I also have a prayer book that I write in every night."**

GCS: Do you have a favorite homemade meal?
B: Probably my mom's baked chicken. It tastes so good. And she makes the crust really crunchy.

GCS: What can't you resist?
B: Cookie-dough ice cream! I like fast food, too, like a chicken sandwich with cheese from Burger King. I just crave that sometimes! And greasy french fries and a Coke. They are so bad for you, but they taste so good!

GCS: What are your fave snacks?
B: I'm a cereal girl – I like Apple Jacks. And macaroni and cheese at night.

GCS: Do you cook?
B: Nope.

GCS: Do you clean up?
B: Yeah, I clean up. I wash the dishes, I vacuum. I clean, make my bed. I do everything!

GCS: You're from a super-small town — Kentwood, La. What's that like?
B: Kentwood has only 1,200 people. But the mall is 30 minutes away, and it's in a bigger city. And it's really cool, though, because where I'm from, you'd think more people would know me — and they do, but they totally respect that I'm trying to lead a somewhat normal life.

GCS: If you go out to the mall with your friends, can you just shop or do you get recognized?
B: It's weird when I go to really big malls because people will notice me. I've been to a couple of malls where it was a bit overwhelming. But my hometown mall is the coolest. No one says anything to me.

Wild & Crazy

GCS: Do you believe in aliens?
B: No.

GCS: Do you read your horoscope?
B: Oh yeah, all the time.

GCS: What's your sign?
B: I'm a Sagittarius.

GCS: What does that mean about you?
B: I travel a lot, which is true. And it's a fire sign, so I have a lot of energy.

GCS: Growing up, did you ever wish your name was something else?
B: Madison. I love the name Madison.

GCS: If you could be invisible for a day, whom would you spy on?
B: My ex-boyfriend…just to see…

GCS: If you could sing a duet with anyone, whom would it be?
B: Ricky Martin. He's very expressive – and he's cute!

GCS: Do you have any special rituals before you perform?
B: I always say a prayer. And I drink a lot of water.

GCS: What's something you heard about yourself that's completely false?
B: The rumors about the breast enlargements and about me dating Justin from *NSync. Both of those rumors are just not true.

GCS: Now that you have fame and fortune, what's been your biggest splurge?
B: A white convertible Mercedes SL 500. My grandmother could get picked up in this car it's so beautiful. (Britney also recently decided to have a bigger house built for her and her family in her hometown.)

GCS: What TV shows do you watch?
B: "Felicity" and "Dawson's Creek."

GCS: What kind of music do you like?
B: Brandy, Lauryn Hill, Whitney Houston, TLC…I like old music, too, like Rick Springfield, John Mellencamp – stuff like that.

GCS: Do you have a favorite movie?
B: "Steel Magnolias." And "Beaches." Those movies make me cry and cry!

GCS: Did you go to your prom?
B: My ex-boyfriend was a senior, so I went to his prom (when I was a freshman). So I've experienced that. The best part of going to the prom is getting ready. You know how the night goes — you go to the dance for 15 minutes and leave, and all you do afterwards is get trashed. I didn't do that, though.

GCS: Finish this sentence: One day I see myself...
B: Eventually there will come a time when I want to settle down and have kids and be completely normal. But that's a long way away, so we'll just have to see!

GCS: What one message do you have for your fans?
B: I'm just being myself, and hopefully that comes across in my music and people dig that. ♥

teenStyle is...

HAIR. BEAUTY. FASHION. ACCESSORIES. CELEBS.

IN EVERY ISSUE...

>> step-by-step celeb hair & makeup looks

>> a-list accessories of the stars

>> hot products hollywood can't live without

>> movie- & music- inspired fashion

>> don't forget the freebie on the cover of every issue!

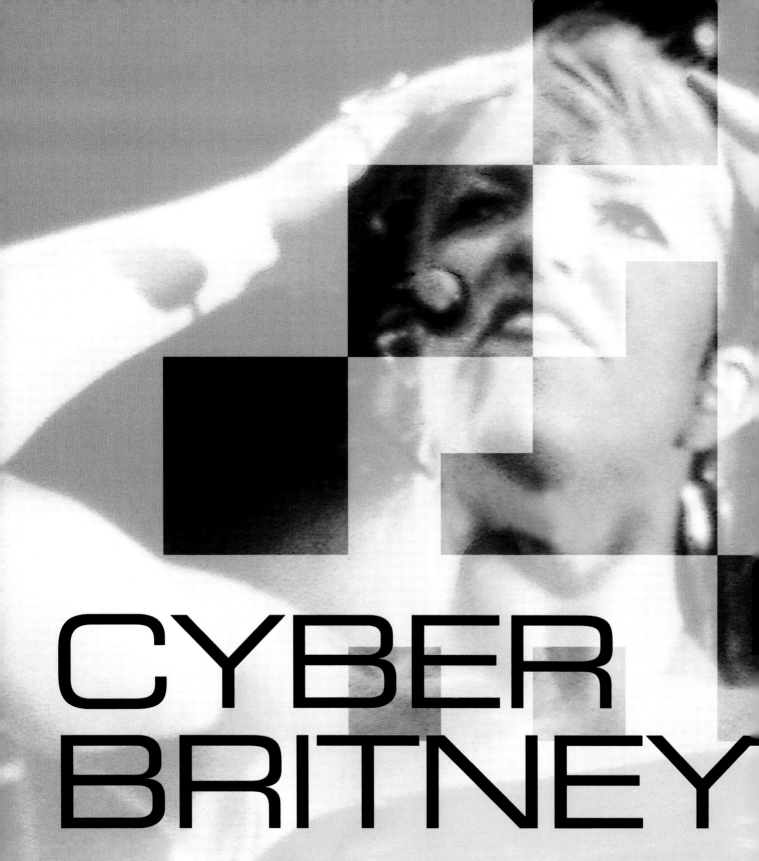

CYBER BRITNEY

She's never met her, talked to her or seen her perform live. But Victoria Masheva has created one of the best Web sites on Britney Spears! How did she do it?

By Michelle Mulder

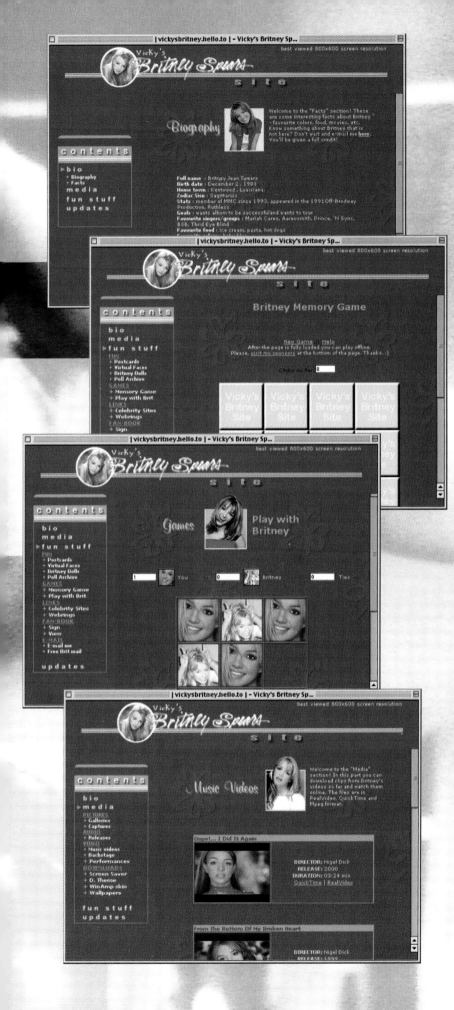

Before we talk to techno wizard Vicky, try this: Do a name search on Yahoo! Enter "Britney Spears" and wait for the results. Surprise! More than 80 Web sites all about Brit will match your inquiry, including Vicky's fan site, http://vicky.britneyzone.com.

That's a HUGE number! So how does somebody make his or her site stand out among all the others? It's no easy task, but Vicky has managed to do just that with plenty of fresh features and cool content. And she does all the work herself!

"Everybody wants to visit sites that have just been updated," said Vicky. "That's why I try to update the site almost every day. I do everything myself, like finding the pictures and videos, plus all of the writing. "

These days, Vicky could be called a Web site expert, as her Britney site illustrates.

Even more amazing – and proving that Britney's popularity is definitely a worldwide phenomenon – is the fact that Vicky lives in Rousse, Bulgaria. She decided to create a Web site about Britney after she saw the video for Britney's first single, "...Baby One More Time," which impressed her with its cool dance scenes and catchy lyrics.

"Honestly, I don't think I'm a HUGE fan," confessed Vicky. "But I like her music and how she dances, probably because I've been dancing for more than eight years."

Since she had never actually designed Web pages before, Vicky used a PC program to help her out. And after many hours of "messing around," she started to get the hang of it. These days, Vicky could be called a Web site expert, as her Britney site illustrates.

Boasting one of the most complete video and audio clip collections on the Web, Vicky's Britney Zone receives 600 to 900 visitors every day! Vicky says she's thrilled the site attracts so many visitors, adding that the best part is the amount of mail she gets from fans. ➜

CYBER BRITNEY

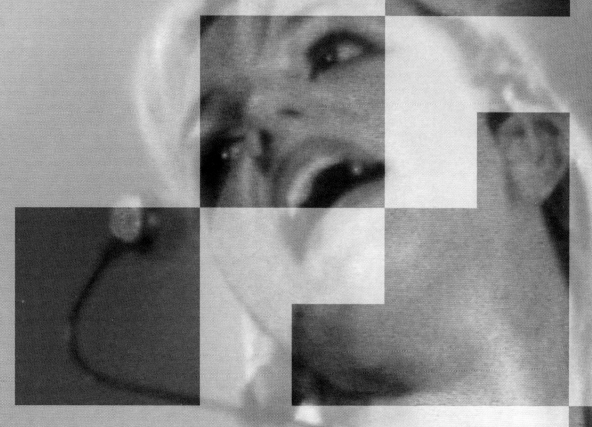

Vicky insists that anyone who has an interest in creating a fan Web site can do it.

"Every day when I open my mail, I always have letters that say, 'I like your site! It's amazing! Keep up the good work!' or something like that," she said. "I like reading that. It makes all my hard work worth the effort knowing that someone likes what I've done."

Vicky says her fave part of the site is the pictures section because "every Britney fan looks for new Britney pics and hot news." To meet that demand, she's always adding new photos of Britney. The more than 500 pictures include shots from overseas magazines that are very hard to find in North America.

Vicky also has updated her Britney video section. Besides the videos for "... Baby One More Time," "Sometimes," "(You Drive Me) Crazy," "From the Bottom of My Broken Heart" and Europe-only release "Born to Make You Happy," clips of some of Brit's live performances and interviews can be found on the site. A recent addition is Britney's performance at the 2000 Grammy Awards.

The site's most unique features include the fun polls and games. You can log on and play a memory game with Britney pics or play a game of tic tac toe with Britney.

Vicky insists that anyone who has an interest in creating a fan site can do it, even if he or she does not have a lot of experience w computers. In fact, Vicky encourages more girls to get into the act.

"Right now, I'm the only PC girl in my class," she said with a l

Vicky also has a little advice for fans who want to create W sites about their fave celebs.

"Be creative and put up your own stuff," said Vicky. "Don take content from other people's sites."

Vicky admits that one of her pet peeves is seeing some of cool, original stuff she's done pop up on other people's Web sit

"I've seen many sites that have copied something from mi she said. "Sure, it means that the Webmaster likes your work, b he or she doesn't even put a link or a credit, that's not cool."

So, after all her hard work, does Vicky ever wonder if Brit has seen her site?

"I hope so and I hope she likes it!" ❤

MORE SPEARS SURFING

Want to know more about your fave pop princess? Check out some of these other cool fan sites dedicated to Britney.

http://www.britney.com

At this official Britney Spears site, you will be guaranteed to find plenty of new and exclusive stuff, including cool contests, the complete 411 on Britney's summer tour and glimpses behind the scenes of Britney's life. The site features a lot of audio and video clips, and you can even remix Britney's hit song "(You Drive Me) Crazy." Drop by and you can download Britney wallpaper and screen savers and join her fan club. This is a must-see site for all Britney fans! ➔

http://www.britney-spears.com

Britney-Spears.com is one of the best places to find the latest Britney news and gossip. Fans from all over the world write in with their latest Britney sightings and info, like the girl who got a glimpse at the new music video being made at Universal Studios! At this site you'll also find a busy chat room and message board and the lyrics to every Britney song. And do you ever wonder about Britney's incredible team of dancers? You can view pictures of them and read their bios here, plus submit your own pictures in the Britney look-a-like section.

http://www.three30.com/pages/britneyonline/

At the recently redesigned Britney Online, you can sign up for a weekly news update about your fave singing sensation or check out the calendar to find out when you can next catch Britney on TV or on tour. Plus, bone up on your Britney knowledge in the bio section. (Did you know her fave drink is Sprite?) And if you're in the mood for a little laughter, make sure to read the site's "Joke of the Week."

http://www.britneyspears.org/

You will be amazed at how much hard-to-get Britney info turns up at BritneySpears.Org every day. From never-before-heard music clips to fan sightings, this site's got the real scoop on Brit. One of the site's top features is the message board, which has plenty of new postings each day.

http://www.britney-spears.ysale.com

This Britney Spears site has all the "need-to-know info" about Britney, including an interview transcript in which she talks about wanting to do a movie and what she really thinks of the Britney Spears dolls (she doesn't like their faces). Plus, check out the childhood pictures of this teen queen. You'll love the too-adorable pic of a barely-walking Britney in a dance recital. And before you go, be sure to browse the picture gallery and send a photo greeting to fellow Britney fans.

http://www.britney-spears.to

With more than 1 million visitors, the "Britney Spears to You" site is probably one of the most-visited on the Web. You can even create your own e-mail account, view backstage videos and send e-postcards to your friends through this site. The chat room is super busy, with fans from all over the world swapping Britney sagas. If you want to brush up on your French or German, try chatting in another language. But beware of Britney bashers who tend to pop up in some of these chat rooms.

http://www.superosity.com/britney/

The creators of "Britney Spears Fan Paradise" claim that the site is constantly updated, so if you want to get up-to-the-minute news about Britney, be sure to check it out. Highlights include the "Random Britney Generator," which alternates between hundreds of Britney photos and an original comic strip. There's also a goofy game for guys called Kiss Britney where boys can choose the just-right pickup line to get Britney to pucker up. ♥

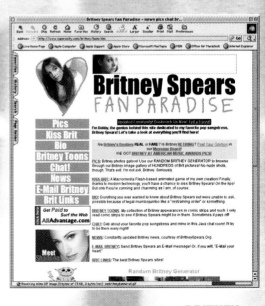

ckin' It!

Britney thrills her fans on tour

CONCERT REVIEW

**Britney Spears
(with LFO and Bosson)
Crazy Tour 2000
New Orleans Arena
New Orleans, La.
Tuesday, April 4, 2000**

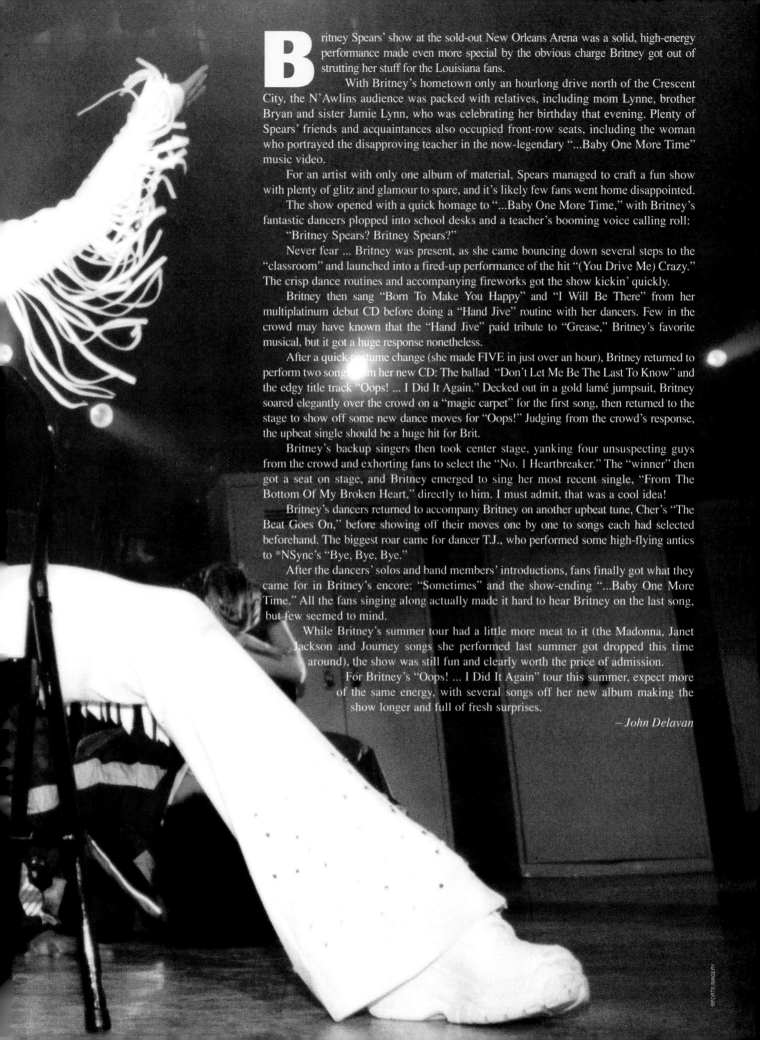

Britney Spears' show at the sold-out New Orleans Arena was a solid, high-energy performance made even more special by the obvious charge Britney got out of strutting her stuff for the Louisiana fans.

With Britney's hometown only an hourlong drive north of the Crescent City, the N'Awlins audience was packed with relatives, including mom Lynne, brother Bryan and sister Jamie Lynn, who was celebrating her birthday that evening. Plenty of Spears' friends and acquaintances also occupied front-row seats, including the woman who portrayed the disapproving teacher in the now-legendary "...Baby One More Time" music video.

For an artist with only one album of material, Spears managed to craft a fun show with plenty of glitz and glamour to spare, and it's likely few fans went home disappointed.

The show opened with a quick homage to "...Baby One More Time," with Britney's fantastic dancers plopped into school desks and a teacher's booming voice calling roll:

"Britney Spears? Britney Spears?"

Never fear ... Britney was present, as she came bouncing down several steps to the "classroom" and launched into a fired-up performance of the hit "(You Drive Me) Crazy." The crisp dance routines and accompanying fireworks got the show kickin' quickly.

Britney then sang "Born To Make You Happy" and "I Will Be There" from her multiplatinum debut CD before doing a "Hand Jive" routine with her dancers. Few in the crowd may have known that the "Hand Jive" paid tribute to "Grease," Britney's favorite musical, but it got a huge response nonetheless.

After a quick costume change (she made FIVE in just over an hour), Britney returned to perform two songs from her new CD: The ballad "Don't Let Me Be The Last To Know" and the edgy title track "Oops! ... I Did It Again." Decked out in a gold lamé jumpsuit, Britney soared elegantly over the crowd on a "magic carpet" for the first song, then returned to the stage to show off some new dance moves for "Oops!" Judging from the crowd's response, the upbeat single should be a huge hit for Brit.

Britney's backup singers then took center stage, yanking four unsuspecting guys from the crowd and exhorting fans to select the "No. 1 Heartbreaker." The "winner" then got a seat on stage, and Britney emerged to sing her most recent single, "From The Bottom Of My Broken Heart," directly to him. I must admit, that was a cool idea!

Britney's dancers returned to accompany Britney on another upbeat tune, Cher's "The Beat Goes On," before showing off their moves one by one to songs each had selected beforehand. The biggest roar came for dancer T.J., who performed some high-flying antics to *NSync's "Bye, Bye, Bye."

After the dancers' solos and band members' introductions, fans finally got what they came for in Britney's encore: "Sometimes" and the show-ending "...Baby One More Time." All the fans singing along actually made it hard to hear Britney on the last song, but few seemed to mind.

While Britney's summer tour had a little more meat to it (the Madonna, Janet Jackson and Journey songs she performed last summer got dropped this time around), the show was still fun and clearly worth the price of admission.

For Britney's "Oops! ... I Did It Again" tour this summer, expect more of the same energy, with several songs off her new album making the show longer and full of fresh surprises.

– John Delavan

live britney

Rosemont, Illinois • Allstate Arena • March 22-23, 2000

britney
live

Tampa, Florida • Ice Palace • March 31, 2000

We ♥ U Britney

#1

BRITNEY Rules!

BRITNEY- I WANT TO Baby!

TOP AND INSET: Britney on "The Tonight Show with Jay Leno"

Britney's live performances always feature myriad costume changes and plenty of high-energy dance routines to keep the fans jumping!

LEFT TO RIGHT: AP/WIDE WORLD (2); STEVE GRANITZ/RETNA; MAX SMITH/RETNA (2)

britney live

Miami, Florida • American Airlines Arena • April 1, 2000

BRITNE
WILL YOU
MARRY ME

BRITNEY
U-DRIVE
ME CRAZY

Arena

Americ

live • britney

Daytona Beach, Florida • Ocean Center • April 2, 2000

HIT ME BRITNEY ONE MORE TIME!

Daytona ♥ you

Britney will soon embark on a huge U.S. summer tour, followed by a three-week tour of Europe with *NSync in October!

live britney

New Orleans, Louisiana • New Orleans Arena • April 4, 2000

Test your B.!Q.

Britney Intelligence Quotient!

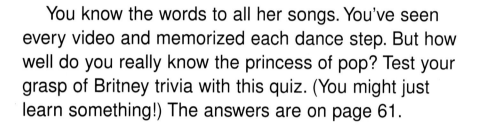

You know the words to all her songs. You've seen every video and memorized each dance step. But how well do you really know the princess of pop? Test your grasp of Britney trivia with this quiz. (You might just learn something!) The answers are on page 61.

1. OK, we'll go easy on you at first: How many years did Britney spend on the Disney Channel's "New Mickey Mouse Club," where so many hot stars got their start?
  a. 1
  b. 2
  c. 3
  d. 4

2. While she was a Mouseketeer, Britney hung out with lots of teens who went on to have pretty impressive careers of their own. Which of these headline-grabbing names did not appear in the *MMC* credits with Britney's?
  a. JC Chasez
  b. Keri Russell
  c. Sarah Michelle Gellar
  d. Justin Timberlake

3. Every girl's got to splurge once in a while. When Britney feels like kicking back in comfy sweats with a big bowl of ice cream, what flavor does she grab?
  a. strawberry
  b. mint chip
  c. chocolate
  d. cookie dough

4. Even though her super-busy life doesn't leave many free minutes for romance, Britney would definitely make time for:
  a. Brad Pitt
  b. James Van Der Beek
  c. Seth Green
  d. Ricky Martin

5. When she's relaxing with family or friends, Britney likes a little TV time. Which of these shows is not one of her must-sees?
  a. "Dawson's Creek"
  b. "Friends"
  c. "The Simpsons"
  d. "Felicity"

6. Britney was one motivated little girl! When she was just 10 years old, she did the theater thing and had a starring role in the off-Broadway show *Ruthless*. What was her character?
  a. a gang gal
  b. a kid who would do anything to be a star
  c. a grouchy cheerleader
  d. a girl who gets even with her best friend for stealing her guy

7. Ever since she was just a kid, this diva has loved music (and singing). You might say she's a natural in the biz. But that songstress urge had to start somewhere, like in the albums she listened to. What's her favorite song from way back when?
  a. "Control"
  b. "Material Girl"
  c. "Sweet Child o' Mine"
  d. "Purple Rain"

8. Britney's hometown of Kentwood, La., is a small place. (Some blocks in New York City have more residents than all of her town!) So traveling to foreign countries took a bit of getting used to for the young star. When Britney boarded her first flight to another country, where was she heading?
  a. Sweden
  b. Japan
  c. France
  d. Great Britain

9. As a major superstar, Britney is beyond popular. Tons of people know who she is, and sometimes that gets kind of weird. The perfect example: What did she find at her home during Christmas in 1998?
- a. a package with an engagement ring from someone she'd never met
- b. an obsessed male fan
- c. a packet of letters from a fourth-grade class in Chicago
- d. a huge teddy bear from a secret admirer

10. All that dancing makes a girl pretty parched. What does she reach for when she needs to quench a burning thirst?
- a. orange juice
- b. Pepsi
- c. Sprite
- d. iced tea

11. Even celebrities have their "most embarrassing moments." What onstage blunder would this star probably like to forget ... but can't?
- a. when she collided with her dancer T.J.
- b. when she ran on stage with her pants unzipped
- c. when she forgot the words to "I Will Still Love You"
- d. when she slipped on a cupcake someone left on the stage

12. Surprise! Britney has bad habits just like everybody else. What bothersome behavior is she trying to conquer?
- a. twirling her hair
- b. never cleaning her room
- c. chewing with her mouth open
- d. biting her nails

13. She may be cute, but Britney's not afraid to break a sweat. Besides dancing up a storm on tour, she likes to swim and take on her brother in a game of one-on-one hoops. She also likes watching basketball on the tube. Which team does she root for?
- a. Chicago Bulls
- b. Los Angeles Lakers
- c. Utah Jazz
- d. Miami Heat

14. Before she hit it big in the music world, Britney did some small-screen time in a bunch of TV commercials. Which of these does not appear on her acting resumé?
- a. a commercial for barbeque sauce
- b. a commercial for a hotel
- c. a commercial for toothpaste
- d. a commercial for a local phone network

15. Nobody can forget Britney's breakout hit "…Baby One More Time." Funny thing is, the song wasn't originally written for her. She got it after another group's record label passed on it. Which group was the song actually written for?
- a. TLC
- b. B*Witched
- c. Spice Girls
- d. Backstreet Boys

16. If you went to Britney's house to hang out, you'd see that her room is full of:
- a. posters of *NSync
- b. a collection of dolls and angels
- c. tons of dried flowers
- d. postcards she's collected from all over the world

17. The song "Soda Pop" (one of her favorites) is part of the soundtrack for what hit TV show?
- a. "Sabrina, the Teenage Witch"
- b. "Buffy the Vampire Slayer"
- c. "Dawson's Creek"
- d. "Felicity"

➜

Test your B.I.Q.
Britney Intelligence Quotient!

18. While Britney's jamming away in the "…Baby One More Time" video, there's a guy in the bleachers who's checking her out. Who is he in real life?
   a. an ex-boyfriend
   b. a good friend she's known since kindergarten
   c. just some random guy
   d. her cousin

19. Back home, Britney's friends have been known to call her by what nickname?
   a. Brit-Brit
   b. Tiny
   c. Britty
   d. Baby

20. When we look at this girl, we can't help thinking she's got incredible style. But even stars have someone they look up to. Who are Britney's favorite fashion icons?
   a. Gwyneth Paltrow and Calista Flockhart
   b. Jennifer Aniston and Jennifer Love Hewitt
   c. Gwen Stefani and Courtney Love
   d. Julia Roberts and Niki Taylor

21. With a red-hot singing career and serious talk about her getting her own television show, what's left for the darling diva? Well, how about the fashion world? Which hip design label has used Britney in ad campaigns?
   a. Rampage
   b. Guess
   c. Tommy Hilfiger
   d. Abercrombie & Fitch

22. Sugar and spice and everything nice … Britney's not that much of a cliché, but like lots of girls she likes to get, well, girlie from time to time. And that includes smelling sweet. What's her favorite scent?
   a. vanilla
   b. juicy berry
   c. lavender
   d. peaches and cream

23. Britney's the first to admit she's a shopaholic. What's the one thing she simply can't resist buying, even though she's already got tons of them?
   a. shoes
   b. lipsticks
   c. comfy cardigans
   d. sunglasses

24. With a December birthday, this babe's a Sagittarius. Sags are what type of sign?
   a. earth
   b. fire
   c. air
   d. water

25. And they're known for being:
   a. sensitive and moody
   b. aggressive, take-charge kind of people
   c. outgoing and cheerful
   d. dreamy homebodies

26. Britney's debut set a serious record. She became the first female artist to have both a debut single and a debut album simultaneously holding down the No. 1 spots on the Billboard charts. On what day was her album released in U.S. stores?
   a. Jan. 1, 1999
   b. Feb. 1, 1999
   c. Jan. 12, 1999
   d. Feb. 14, 1999

27. With all of the traveling she's done, Britney didn't keep the same school schedule most of her friends did. Still, she realized how important education is, and she does plan to go to college someday. When she hits the books, what's her favorite subject?
   a. math
   b. history
   c. art
   d. English

28. Like we said, there's nothing this girl likes better than a day of shopping. (It kind of fits that her first tour took her through the malls of America!) Which of these stores is not one of her favorite places to spend a little cash?
   a. Contempo Casuals
   b. The Gap
   c. Bebe
   d. A/X

29. If she's in the mood for a good chick flick, which of these is Britney most likely to pop into the VCR?
   a. Beauty and the Beast
   b. Pretty Woman
   c. Ever After
   d. Steel Magnolias

30. And something silly and simple to wrap it all up: What's Britney's favorite color?
   a. hot pink
   b. baby blue
   c. bright red
   d. pale purple ♥

SCORE YOUR QUIZ

23 to 30 points
So when is your Britney biography going to be published?

You know enough about the talented Ms. Spears to fill a book. Whether it's her favorite movie or the snack she likes to chomp, you've got the answers nailed. Clearly, this star is one of your favorites, and you're always up on the latest Britney trivia, like who she's seeing and when she's performing. If we had to guess, we'd say your room is probably full of books about her, and you've probably been known to wear some of her signature looks.

16 to 22 points
Pick a fact, any fact.

You've been on the Britney bandwagon since day one, and you're pretty well read when it comes to this singing sensation. You've even been known to buy new Britney mags whenever you see them at the newsstand. But no matter how much you like to find out new stuff about her life, you're interested in lots of other things, too. In fact, you've got the best of both worlds: You can have a blast as a fabulous fan and enjoy being a teenage girl without getting lost in Britney mania. But hey, you wouldn't say no to concert tickets ...

9 to 15 points
Sort of Spears savvy

You love her songs and watch her videos. You read about her when you can, but you don't go out of your way to load up on factoids about Britney's life and loves. Frankly, there are too many other things out there vying for your attention. If you ever feel at a loss when your friends start swapping the latest celeb gossip, just change the subject. (If it really gets to you, you can always try reading a few extra articles about the pop princess. That will get you in the know in no time.)

0 to 8 points
Britney who?

You might think you're a Britney scholar, but your score says something else. You obviously have an interest in the diva or you wouldn't have bought this magazine, but you've got a long way to go before you can consider yourself an expert on her life. Maybe you just started listening to her music, or maybe you just haven't made an effort to get to know the girl behind the songs. You can still have a great time singing along, just don't bet your friends that you know more about Brit-Brit than they do.

FLASH

Even before hitting it big with "...Baby One

By David Fantle and Tom Johnson

Few entertainers had as good a year as Britney Spears did in 1999.

Her debut CD, "...Baby One More Time," hit No. 1 on the *Billboard* album chart, and it has gone on to sell an astonishing 12 million copies in the United States alone. She staged her first world tour and released several hit singles, including "Sometimes" and "(You Drive Me) Crazy." →

BACK!

re Time," Britney was destined to be a star.

destined to be a star

Southern Belle

Unlike some male pop artists who have enjoyed success with a mostly female fan base, Britney is proving popular with fans of both genders.

"Guys are into her because she's cute, and girls like her because she's not trying too hard," was how *NSync's JC Chasez, a friend of Britney's, described her appeal to *People*.

But ask fans like 17-year-old Jake Zarling, who lives in suburban Milwaukee, and he's even more direct.

"She's hot!," he exclaimed.

Jake has even reserved a coveted place in his bedroom (right above his bed's headboard) for a poster of his favorite star. This is no small accomplishment for Britney, since her poster shares the room with a dresser-top full of athletic trophies, team banners and photos of his all-male sports heroes — Michael Jordan and Green Bay Packers quarterback Brett Favre.

Jake's sentiments are clearly shared by the large contingent of young males who attend Britney's sold-out shows.

While Britney's appeal is highest with teenage fans, her singable, danceable music has also caught on with toddlers, much to the confusion of young parents, most of whom ask, "Britney who?" At a recent dance class of mostly preschool and elementary school girls, the *Honolulu Advertiser* noted that the kids had no interest in moving to the beat of Barney or the Teletubbies. When asked whom they wanted to groove to, they collectively screamed, "Britney Spears! Britney Spears!"

So how did this young superstar get her start?

Britney Jean Spears was born on Dec. 1, 1981, in the small Louisiana town of Kentwood (population 2,500), about an hourlong drive north of New Orleans. Her father, Jamie, works in the construction trade and her mother, Lynne, is a second-grade schoolteacher. Britney has a 22-year-old brother, Bryan (a sports administration major at Southwest Mississippi Community College), and a 9-year-old sister, Jamie Lynn. A rambunctious toddler, Britney was given the nickname Brit-Brit.

Britney never disses her hometown, although she jokingly told an online chat audience, "It's not very hip at all. You have to travel 30 minutes just to get to McDonald's."

By all accounts, Britney's childhood in Kentwood was normal and included regular church-going (she's a Baptist), a practice she continues today.

"I still try to get to church even when I'm traveling," she said. "But I have my Bible and say my prayers every night."

Kentwood's most famous export took a shine to performing at age 2, when she began singing and dancing for imaginary audiences. At age 5, she sang "What Child Is This?" at her kindergarten graduation.

"She would put on makeup and sing to herself in the bathroom mirror," brother Bryan told *People*.

"I would get on my mom's nerves," added Britney. "When I was a little girl, I was always performing. I remember buying 'Thriller' (Michael Jackson's mega-hit album), and I used to dance around the room all the time. I probably drove my mom mad. She must have thought she had a problem child. But I didn't get into show business because I've got a pushy mother.

BRITNEY'S SCHOOL DAYS! *From left to right: Britney (left) named "Junior High Beauty" at Parklane Academy in McComb, Miss., in 1997; Britney (second from right) in her Algebra I class; Britney (left) as freshman year homeroom secretary; posing with Mason Statham in 1996 "Junior High Most Beautiful" photo; Britney (left, No. 25) on the junior varsity basketball team; Britney's "Junior High Who's Who" photo in 1997; young Britney named 7th grade "Class Favorite"; Britney as freshman maid in the 1997 Homecoming Court.*

She's not one of those stage moms. It was always me who wanted to do all of the performing."

Added Britney to CNN: "I was actually really obnoxious. I was always singing to the radio and always dancing and doing my own thing. My mother took me to a dance instructor. All she did was teach dance, but she told my mother, 'Your daughter can sing. Why don't you start entering her in singing and dancing contests?' One thing led to another and things my mom thought were really obnoxious turned out to be really cool."

While mimicking the Whitney Houston and Mariah Carey hits she listened to constantly, Britney developed her distinctive singing style.

As a child, Britney told *Twist*, "I had moods where I just wanted to get on the go-cart – that's not a girlie thing to do. But then I'd have moments where I'd go into my playhouse and play dolls for six hours."

At age 8, to supplement her dancing lessons, Britney took up gymnastics and briefly attended Bela Karolyi's training camp.

Meeting 'The Mouse'

At age 9, Britney learned that The Disney Channel was holding auditions in Atlanta for its revival of the '50s *Mickey Mouse Club*. While she made a positive impression on the producers, Britney was deemed too young and received her walking papers. It was to be a rare taste of rejection for the up-and-coming star. Nevertheless, an astute producer still helped Britney, who was simply too young for the Disney show, secure an agent.

Undaunted, and now with her parents' full support, Britney, her mom and little sister Jamie Lynn moved to New York City's rugged Hell's Kitchen neighborhood to help nurture Britney's artistic talents. For the next three summers, Britney honed her skills at the prestigious Off-Broadway Dance Center and the Professional Performing Arts School. She also began landing spots for national TV commercials and Off-Broadway shows, including the 1991 comedy, *Ruthless*, based on the 1956 thriller *The Bad Seed*.

"At 10, I was playing this really bad child who seems real sweet... but she's evil, too," said Britney. "It was so much fun." The 10-year-old Britney was also a *Star Search* winner.

Britney took the move to New York in stride.

"I was really thankful because you know most parents push the child," she said. "I was the one who was pushing. I'm from a small town and people were like, 'You're sending your daughter to New York? Are you crazy?' But I was the one who wanted to do it and I'm thankful because they were so supportive.

"I really didn't like (New York City) at first," she added. "And my mom was like, 'Baby, whenever you want to go home, we'll go.'"

At age 11, she now had the maturity and credentials to audition again for *The New Mickey Mouse Club*, although she remained the show's youngest performer. She landed a coveted spot and for the next two years had mouse ears almost permanently attached to her head.

"(Being a Mouseketeer) was a lot of fun because I ➜

SETH POPPEL YEARBOOK ARCHIVES (8)

was like a baby," she told an online chat audience. "I was 11 or 12 and was the youngest one on the show, so people catered to me. Just being in Disney World alone was a lot of fun. There were about 20 kids with me; I just loved it there. It's still my favorite place to go, just like everyone else. I mean, it's Disney World for heaven's sake!"

Making Music

While performing for *The New Mickey Mouse Club*, Britney realized she wanted to pursue a career in music. Britney's class of fellow Mouseketeers also included future stars Keri Russell of TV's *Felicity* and JC Chasez and Justin Timberlake of *NSync.

After performing on the show for two years, Britney, now 14, handed in her mouse ears and returned to Kentwood for one normal year at high school. She actually attended a private high school, Park Lane Academy in nearby McComb, Miss. But Britney, who now had a taste of stardom, felt stifled by the school's strict rules. She compared her situation to the opening scene in the movie *Clueless* – with all the cliques, from the cheerleaders and jocks, to the burnouts.

Britney's mom, Lynne, told *People*, "Going into the middle of the year, she was antsy."

Added Britney: "I did the homecoming and the prom thing, and I was totally bored. ... I started getting itchy to get out again

and see the world. I need to sing, and I love to travel."

The aforementioned prom date was with a young man named Reg, whom Britney says was her only real boyfriend to date. The two were together for two years before Britney's budding career and frequent road trips put the relationship on ice.

"It wasn't that I was changing," Britney said of the breakup. "We broke up before any of my success had happened. He became insecure about himself, I felt. I wasn't gonna do anything. I'm a straight-up, honest person, and if I was gonna do anything, I'd tell him before I'd do it and end the relationship. I was really head over heels in love. I don't think I'll ever love somebody like that again. I just woke up one day, and click, it was gone."

Britney maintained her studies by enrolling in a University of Nebraska home schooling program. "I worry about her terribly," Lynne said. "But I'm so much happier knowing she's doing what she really wants to do."

Rolling Stone describes her ranch-style home this way: "Britney's 'girly' bedroom, like the rest of her house, is awash in floral patterns and frills."

Now a seasoned performer, an audition for an all-girl vocal group led to her developing a solo career as a pop singer as well as continuing her high school studies with tutors.

"I need a lot of help in geometry and Spanish," she said. "I know I've had to give up stuff to do this, but I don't miss high school. When I was home, every weekend we'd go out and do the same thing. It's wonderful as long as you love what you're doing, but I'd rather be doing this!"

When Britney turned 15, Lynne sent a homemade demo tape of her daughter to Larry Rudolph, a well-connected New York City entertainment lawyer. He became her co-manager and soon signed Britney to a recording contract with Jive Records.

After auditioning for a Jive executive by singing "Jesus Loves Me" and Whitney Houston's "I Have Nothing," Jive

BRITNEY SPEARS THROUGH THE YEARS! *From left to right: Britney's 1st grade photo in 1989; her 2nd grade photo in 1990; her 3rd grade photo in 1991; Britney's 6th grade photo in 1994; Britney named "Junior High Beauty" in 7th grade in 1995; Britney in her 8th grade photo in 1996; her freshman year class photo in 1997; Britney looks all grown up in 1998.*

Records chief Barry Weiss signed the 15-year-old and shipped her off to Sweden to craft her debut album with writer/producer Max Martin, the man with the golden touch behind the music of Backstreet Boys.

Food Court Queen

Superstardom did not come overnight. With no recording to promote, Britney did what other pop stars, such as Debbie Gibson and Tiffany, did before her: She headlined at shopping malls throughout the country. Unsuspecting parents taking their teenage kids to the Gap and Old Navy were suddenly curious onlookers, diverted to an attractive young teenager belting out pop tunes in the middle of the mall. As the mall tour grew, so did the size of her audience. It wasn't long before poor Britney was being mauled by fans at malls nationwide.

It was a dicey career move, especially considering that the careers of Gibson and Tiffany quickly crashed, but Britney didn't seem to care.

"It was crazy," she told *People*. "No one knew who I was, but I could see that they really enjoyed the music. And I got a lot of shopping done!"

The Big Break

Little did Britney know what was in store for her when in 1998, she went into the recording studio to lay down the tracks for her debut album, "...Baby One More Time."

The next chapter of her life was about to begin, and there would be no looking back. ❤

SETH POPPEL YEARBOOK ARCHIVES (7)

Lookin' Go

Take a peek inside Britney's beauty bag and learn how to steal her style

Whether she's on MTV's "TRL," dancing in her latest video or performing on tour or at an awards show, Britney Spears always looks absolutely fabulous from head to toe. The designer duds she shows up in may cost big bucks, but her fave beauty products are in everyone's price range. Check out the six indulgences Britney swears by.

The Body Shop Lipsticks

"I absolutely love these shimmer lipsticks," said Britney. "The Body Shop has the best ones."

"I'll use a little Clinique toner after I wash my face to tighten up my pores. It makes my face feel clean."

PRODUCT PHOTOS BY DENNIS JORDAN PHOTOGRAPHY, OPPOSITE PAGE: TOP TO BOTTOM: MARC BAPTISTE/OUTLINE, MATTHEW JORDAN SMITH/OUTLINE, JOHN BARRETT/GLOBE, NINA PROMMER/GLOBE. THIS PAGE: JON RAGEL/OUTLINE

Lookin' Good

Vanilla Lace perfume by Victoria's Secret
"I love vanilla!" Enough said.

Clinique Clarifying Lotion 2
"I'll use a little Clinique toner after I wash my face to tighten up my pores. It makes my face feel clean."

Bath & Body Works Moisture-Rich Body Lotion in Vanilla Bean
"If there's one thing I really love, it's the lotions from Bath & Body Works. They're really, really thick."

Feel Perfecte Foundation by L'Oréal
"After I use the toner, I'll put this on. It makes your face look flawless. And it's made from the same company as Lancôme — it's just $15 cheaper."

The Body Shop Eyeshadows
"I love browns. I'll use a darker one on my lid and a lighter one on my browbone."

"If there's one thing I really love, it's the lotions from Bath & Body Works."

PRODUCED/WRITTEN BY DENNIS JOURDAN PHOTOGRAPHY THIS PAGE: RAUHAUSER/BILODEAU/ME

Warmin' Up

LFO

These up-and-coming artists hype the crowd before Britney takes the stage

By Linda Twardowski

NOT LONG AGO, POP STAR BRITNEY SPEARS WAS just another gifted but unknown talent cheerfully schlepping her vocal chords and dance steps from shopping mall to shopping mall. But with the release of one multiplatinum album, another CD in stores now and dozens of sold-out concerts crossed off this teen's to-do list, you might think Miss Spears would be glad to put her underdog days behind her.

Britney, however, refuses to rest on her laurels.

*NSync gave Britney a big break when the group offered her an opening-act slot in late 1998. Now, Britney is returning the favor by inviting a variety of talented acts to go on the road with her. By hooking up some of her deserving industry peers with the most important people she knows – her fans – Britney is giving these up-and-comers some super exposure.

Shortly after her opening gig for *NSync, Britney watched as her first single and album went to No. 1. Then she embarked on her first headlining tour in the summer of 1999. In just over three months, Britney's voice would carry her from Pompano Beach, Fla. to Allentown, Pa., with stops in every fan-filled place from the Six Flags amusement parks in St. Louis and Dallas to the New York State Fair in Syracuse.

Yep, the little girl from Louisiana had made it. But just because Britney had become a music industry mega-star, she wasn't above giving other promising acts the same boost *NSync had given her. So who were the lucky acts to receive the invite of a lifetime? Read on to find out who has already been on the road with Britney and who will be on tour with her this summer! →

Britney started her singing career as an opening act. Now she's returning the favor by giving artists like LFO (left) opening act slots on her tours.

Michael Fredo

Michael Fredo wowed fans on Britney's Summer 1999 U.S. tour.

t's a well-known fact among Britney fans that the pop star's fave outfits and perfume come courtesy of Tommy Hilfiger's line. So when the Hilfiger family – specifically, Andy Hilfiger, head of the new record label Andy Hilfiger Entertainment – came knocking at the superstar's stage door with a somewhat different design, Britney had to take a look. No doubt, she's glad she did. Andy Hilfiger offered up his latest project: Michael Fredo.

Michael, a talented musician and vocalist, had been singing since he was 8 years old. He started like any pop star from Britney to Whitney, singing in church choirs. When his soprano chords matured with age, Fredo joined a folk group, then went on to perform with rock 'n roll bands while he was still in high school. By his senior year, Michael knew music was his calling, so he enrolled in The Professional Children's School in New York and began studying classical music. His studies paid off as Michael later went on the road as a jazz vocalist for the esteemed Ellington Orchestra.

Sound a bit misdirected for a soon-to-be pop phenomenon? Ha! Listen to Michael's debut CD, "Introducing," and you'll know: That isn't the sound of misdirection you're hearing; that's a well-schooled fusion of stirring sounds, smart lyrics and wild styles.

"I call it youthquake – a new form of pop music that mixes a lot of different styles."

"I call it youthquake – a new form of pop music that mixes a lot of different styles," said Michael. He would know: In addition to playing guitar and piano on "Introducing," Michael also wrote four of the songs, and on the others he collaborated with his label president, Andy Hilfiger, and Qwest Records' Quincy Jones, famed producer for legends like Michael Jackson. The result?

An album that combines upbeat rock, soulful ballads and dance-floor pop.

Since completing "Introducing" and going on Britney's tour last summer, Michael has been in high demand. He performed at a VH1 benefit concert for multiple sclerosis with artists such as the Goo Goo Dolls, Coolio and LL Cool J, and he popped up in some national commercials for Tommy Jeans.

Boyz N Girlz United

So what do a certified black belt in Tae Kwon Do, an ex-bag boy at Publix, an accident-prone dancer and a fast-car hobbyist have in common? Well, if you're talking about the four talented members of Boyz N Girlz United, two things: Big dreams and bigger realities.

First, their dreams: The New York-born, Orlando-transplanted Criss Ruiz liked her black belt just fine, but wanted to follow in her doo-wop daddy's footsteps and get her chops as a singer. As for Daniel Dix, since wowing his church at age 5, the Cape Canaveral, Fla., native had the same goal and wasn't willing to bag it for a higher position at Publix.

Rina Mayo, a Houston gal with Broadway dreams, wasn't about to let five broken bones get in her way: Singing and dancing earned her far more pleasure than pain. And as for West Virginia's Robbie Carrico, shaping the fine fiberglass lines of Porsches and Vipers was cool, but his road was leading to a place where his hip-hop and street-jazz styles of dance set the pace.

So where did they all end up? Together, in Boyz N Girlz United. The group started after Criss and Rina's two-gal harmony caught the attention of acclaimed *NSync and Britney Spears manager Johnny Wright's management company, Wright Entertainment Group (WEG). It was clear the talented vocal and dance duo made a fab team, but Criss and Rina wanted to go one better – or

would that be two better? – by expanding their sound into a four-part harmony. With support from WEG, the girls began scouting the Orlando talent circuit.

Months later, Rina and her mom spotted a surefire star at a local dance competition: Robbie. Of the shocking invitation to audition for Boyz N Girlz United that followed, Robbie said, "It was so out of the blue!" But apparently it was as good as gold. Robbie was asked to sign on and soon after, Rina and Robbie spied Daniel belting out his rendition of Joe Cocker's "You Are So Beautiful" at the Cocoa High School talent pageant. Besides sweeping the show and winning the title of Mr. Cocoa High, Daniel nabbed another honor: He completed the four-star group, Boyz N Girlz United.

Enter reality: Since banding together, the four dreamers have roused

the crowds during Britney's 1999 summer tour; watched their first single, "Messed Around," gain popularity on the radio; and wrapped up work on their self-titled debut album (set to hit stores this summer). The CD's urban jams, achy ballads and disco-saturated tunes are certainly something the group can be proud of.

Besides co-writing some of the album's lyrics, the group made a concerted effort to keep the feel real – something they know their audience appreciates.

"We've all had our puppy-love crushes and dreamed about somebody," said Rina. "We just wanted to make music that other kids our age can understand. I just hope that everybody likes the music and has fun with it because we sure are. We're having a great time." ➜

"We just wanted to make music that other kids our age can understand."

● Left to right: Rina Mayo, Robbie Carrico, Criss Ruiz and Daniel Dix

LFO

As one of the latest confections from Orlando-based hit-maker Lou Pearlman's Transcontinental Entertainment — yep, the same guy partly responsible for the sweet successes seen by *NSync and Backstreet Boys — LFO wants nothing more than to stand apart from the rest.

Well, they've got their wish. And it has nothing to do with the fact that each member of the group towers over 6 feet tall. Rich Cronin, Brad Fischetti and Devin Lima make a point to stand head and shoulders above most other young, male acts thanks to their talents. Not only do the guys write and produce their own material, they don't rest until they've mixed an eclectic bunch of funk, rap, humor, pop and originality into each song.

Their first single, the funky radio anthem "Summer Girls," gave listeners a taste of their clever capabilities: Can lines like "Fell deep in love, but now we ain't speakin'/ Michael J. Fox was Alex P. Keaton" show anything but? That prompted Backstreet Boys, *NSync and LL Cool J to invite LFO to warm up the audiences for their concerts. In true LFO fashion, the boys went one better, burning up the stage with their hot-performance style, then retreating into the recording studios to fire up the teary-eyed ballads and kitschy funk songs they'd perfected for their debut album, LFO. By the time it reached stores, fans were screaming for more from the "Lyte Funkie Ones."

The Britney Spears camp wasted little time in heeding the fans' call. They snatched up LFO for the second leg of Britney's North American tour that began March 8, 2000, in Pensacola, Fla. How's it going thus far? According to fans and critics alike, LFO has a bright future. Of course, that's no news to the boys.

"When you see what comes next," said Brad, "you'll be mesmerized." ➔

"When you see what comes next," said Brad, "you'll be mesmerized."

Brad Fischetti

Devin Lima

Rich Cronin

Check out LFO on Nickelodeon's All That and More Tour this summer!

BBMak

You may not have heard of BBMak yet, but you will. The up-and-coming British trio, who will be touring with Britney Spears in June and July, is already a hit overseas. The group's single, "Back Here," reached No. 1 in Japan, and the guys just finished a successful stint on the "Smash Hits" tour in the United Kingdom.

Made up of Christian Burns, Mark Barry and Ste McNally, BBMak makes music that combines elements of pop, rock and soul.

"When you hear BBMak, what you're hearing is actually our personalities," said Christian. "It's not a record company's ideas. It's actually us that comes out in the melodies, the lyrics and the production."

Four years ago, Christian, Mark and Ste were playing in different bands around northwest England. They later teamed up, writing most of their own music and producing their own songs, along with playing their instruments and singing.

Ste played guitar for a band as a teenager, but didn't think about singing until he joined BBMak.

"When I met Mark and Christian, they encouraged me to sing," he said.

Ste is also the one who came up with the group's name.

"I just took the first initials from our (last) names, and that's how I came up with it," he said.

Mark got his musical start on the bagpipes at age 10. He also has a passion for singing and cites superstars like Donnie Hathaway, Stevie Wonder and the Jackson 5 as his inspirations.

"The influence for me is soul," said Mark. "Christian's more of the pop side, and Ste's got the rock side. So with the three of us together, you get the soul with the harmonies, the rock with the production and the pop with the melodies. It's a good mixture."

Christian, BBMak's rhythm guitarist, began playing at age 14. He cites the Beatles, the Eagles and Billy Joel as some of his influences.

BBMak has been going full speed ahead since finishing the "Smash Hits" tour, with an appearance on the Disney Channel special, "M2M and BBMak in Concert," on April 29, and the group's debut album, "Sooner or Later," hitting the United States on May 16, the same day as Britney's new album.

To check out BBMak online, visit www.bbmak.com.

Left to right: Mark Barry, Christian Burns and Ste McNally

Bosson

For the Swedish-born Staffan "Bosson" Olsson, the road to fame in the music industry might have been a long one – he began singing at age 6 – but when one travels at warp speed, the ride is considerably more exciting. And since 1999, warp speed is exactly where this Swede's odometer has been set.

Backtrack just a bit to December of 1998. Bosson, then supported by the Swedish indie label MNW Dance, was home in his Gothenburg apartment, while just across the ocean, executives from MNW were spinning their wares for Terry Anzalado, one half of the powerhouse team that makes up Good Guy Entertainment. Disc after disc twirled 'round the turntable with little recognition from Terry, until Bosson's track "We Live" started pumping.

As Terry told Gavin.com, "It was like ear candy." And Good Guys Entertainment was hungry for more.

Terry soon was out the door and on the horn with his partner, and soon after, the composer/producer/vocalist Bosson was back in Sweden. Good Guys Entertainment signed Bosson, asking that he continue writing songs in Sweden while the company worked to spread his unique sound inside American borders. The work turned out to be pretty easy. Despite the fact that Bosson wasn't even signed to an American record label yet, Los Angeles radio station KIIS-FM picked up the single in a matter of weeks, and persistent call-ins from listeners proved Bosson was a hit.

Of course, that was no surprise to Europe as fans in Norway, Spain, Greece and Lithuania had been following Bosson since he toured as part of the popular trio Elevate between 1993 and 1996. Now, as a soloist, Bosson was finding the same recognition here in the United States. Capitol Records cut him a deal, and in return, Bosson gave Capitol an album, "One In A Million." Though the much-talked-about CD won't

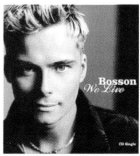

hit stores until the summer of 2000, Bosson is already tearing things up around the country as he tours with Britney this spring.

So has his tornado-speed catapult from relative unknown to spotlight-sharing rocker given this rising star a serious case of jet lag? Maybe, but while his estimated time of arrival might have come quicker than he dared hope, to hear Bosson tell it, he's quite happy with his chosen destination.

"I love to perform on stage, to get to an audience, to entertain them, joke with them – it doesn't matter what I have to do to make them happy, make them feel good," said Bosson. "The kick I get back when they sing my song ... that response is everything."

A*Teens

A*Teens, a hot new teen group from Sweden, also recently landed a spot on Britney's summer tour. From July 19 through Aug. 14, the group will show off its high-energy tunes to America!

Several classic dance songs get a new spin on the A*Teens' debut album, "The ABBA Generation," which was scheduled for release May 23. The single "Dancing Queen" – a hit for the group ABBA in 1977 – went No. 1 on Radio Disney in April.

The group consists of four teens – Marie Serneholt, 16; Sara Lumholdt, 15; Dhani Lennevald, 15; and Amit Paul, 16.

They're already super popular in their native Sweden and look forward to a U.S. invasion with their ABBA remakes.

"It's a lot of fun singing and dancing to ABBA songs," said Marie. "To mix contemporary music styles with ABBA's fantastic material is exciting. We look at A*Teens as a tribute to ABBA." ❤

Left to right: Marie Serneholt, Amit Paul, Sarah Lumholdt and Dhani Lennevald

BRITNEY HITS THE ROAD

As beautiful as Britney Spears is, it's obvious she still doesn't get much beauty sleep! Only two months after her "Crazy Tour 2000" (featuring opening acts LFO and Bosson) wrapped up in Charleston, W.Va., Britney launches her "Oops! ... I Did It Again! Tour" in Charlotte, N.C. She will be on the road throughout North America until after Labor Day, hitting such hot spots as Las Vegas' MGM Grand Garden and the legendary Hollywood Bowl in Los Angeles.

If you've seen Britney perform live, then you know what to expect: Lots of high-energy dance numbers with a few tender ballads thrown in to give Britney's dancers a breather! You can also expect to hear most of the songs off Britney's

new album since she only performed two of them – title track "Oops! ... I Did It Again!" and "Don't Let Me Be The Last To Know" – during the "Crazy Tour 2000" in March and April.

Tickets for all of these concerts went on sale several weeks ago, so many shows are already sold out. Still, you should check the day of the show to see if any additional tickets are released at the venue closest to you. You can also check Web sites like www.tickets.com or www.ticketsnow.com, but be forewarned: tickets purchased through those sites will probably cost a lot more than face value!

For updates to this list of shows, check www.pollstar.com or www.ticketmaster.com.

BRITNEY SPEARS' SUMMER 2000 TOUR

* Note: All dates and venues are subject to change

DATE(S)	CITY	VENUE
Thursday, June 15	Charlotte, N.C.	Blockbuster Pavilion
Friday, June 16	Raleigh, N.C.	Alltel Pavilion at Walnut Creek
Saturday, June 17	Virginia Beach, Va.	GTE Virginia Beach Amphitheater
Sunday, June 18	Bristow, Va.	Nissan Pavilion
Tuesday, June 20	Columbia, Md.	Merriweather Post Pavilion
Wednesday, June 21	Hartford, Conn.	Meadows Music Theatre
Friday, June 23	Darien Center, N.Y.	Darien Lake Six Flags
Saturday, June 24	Hershey, Pa.	Hershey Park Stadium
Sunday, June 25	Scranton, Pa.	Montage Mountain
Tuesday-Thursday, June 27-29	Wantagh, N.Y.	Jones Beach Amphitheatre
Sunday-Monday, July 2-3	Holmdel, N.J.	PNC Bank Arts Center
Wednesday, July 5	Camden, N.J.	Blockbuster-Sony Entertainment Centre
Friday, July 7	Tinley Park, Ill.	New World Music Theatre
Saturday, July 8	Milwaukee	Marcus Amphitheater
Sunday-Monday, July 9-10	Clarkston, Mich.	Pine Knob Music Theatre
Sunday, July 16	Maryland Heights, Mo.	Riverport Amphitheatre
Monday, July 17	Bonner Springs, Kan.	Sandstone Amphitheatre
Wednesday, July 19	Dallas	Starplex Amphitheatre
Thursday, July 20	San Antonio	Alamodome
Friday-Saturday, July 21-22	The Woodlands, Texas	C.W. Mitchell Pavilion
Wednesday, July 26	Denver	Red Rocks Amphitheatre
Thursday, July 27	Albuquerque, N.M.	Mesa Del Sol Amphitheatre
Friday, July 28	Phoenix	Blockbuster Desert Sky Pavilion
Saturday, July 29	Irvine, Calif.	Irvine Meadows Amphitheatre
Monday, July 31	Los Angeles	Hollywood Bowl
Tuesday, Aug. 1	Concord, Calif.	Chronicle Pavilion at Concord
Thursday, Aug. 3	San Diego	San Diego Sports Arena
Friday, Aug. 4	Las Vegas	MGM Grand Garden
Saturday, Aug. 5	Devore, Calif.	G.H. Blockbuster Pavilion
Sunday, Aug. 6	Marysville, Calif.	Sacramento Valley Amphitheatre
Tuesday, Aug. 8	Mountain View, Calif.	Shoreline Amphitheatre
Thursday, Aug. 10	Portland, Ore.	Rose Garden
Friday, Aug. 11	Seattle	Gorge Amphitheatre
Saturday, Aug. 12	Vancouver, B.C.	General Motors Place
Monday, Aug. 14	Salt Lake City	Delta Center
Monday, Aug. 21	Burgettstown, Pa.	Post-Gazette Pavilion at Star Lake
Tuesday, Aug. 22	Toronto	Molson Amphitheatre
Monday, Aug. 28	Mansfield, Mass.	Tweeter Center for the Performing Arts
Wednesday, Aug. 30	Saratoga Springs, N.Y.	Saratoga Performing Arts Center
Thursday, Aug. 31	Cleveland	Gund Arena
Friday, Sept. 1	Knoxville, Tenn.	Thompson-Boling Arena
Saturday, Sept. 2	Noblesville, Ind.	Deer Creek Music Center
Sunday, Sept. 3	Columbus, Ohio	Polaris Amphitheater
Tuesday, Sept. 5	Nashville, Tenn	AmSouth Amphitheatre
Wednesday, Sept. 6	Atlanta	Lakewood Amphitheatre
Saturday, Sept. 9	Orlando, Fla.	TD Waterhouse Centre
Sunday, Sept. 10	West Palm Beach, Fla.	Mars Music Amphitheatre

GET THE GOODS

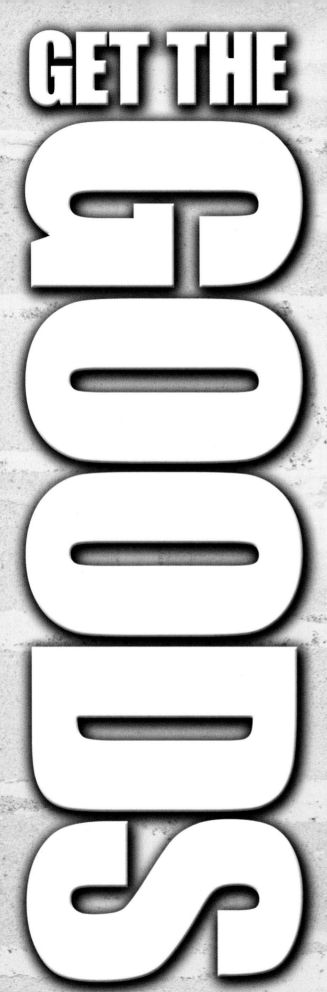

Be prepared to empty your piggy bank if you want to own all of Britney's CDs and other cool stuff

Even the most devoted Britney Spears fan would face a huge challenge trying to collect all of Britney's CDs and other Britney-related items. In just under two years in the international spotlight, Britney has released a flood of merchandise, from full-length compact discs (and hard-to-find CD singles) to Britney dolls, home videos, posters, books and bubble gum.

"Britney mania" is a worldwide phenomenon, and with Britney's sophomore album hitting stores now, don't expect it to end anytime soon! How many of her CDs and other items do you own?

Britney Spears Discography
FULL-LENGTH ALBUMS

...Baby One More Time
Release Date: Jan. 12, 1999
Track Listing
01. ...Baby One More Time
02. (You Drive Me) Crazy
03. Sometimes
04. Soda Pop
05. Born To Make You Happy
06. From The Bottom Of My Broken Heart
07. I Will Be There
08. I Will Still Love You (featuring Don Philip)
09. Thinkin' About You
10. E-Mail My Heart
11. The Beat Goes On

Oops! ... I Did It Again
Release Date: May 16, 2000
1. Oops! ... I Did It Again
2. Stronger
3. Don't Go Knockin' On My Door
4. Satisfaction (I Can't Get No)
5. Don't Let Me Be The Last To Know
6. What U See (Is What U Get)
7. Lucky
8. One Kiss From You
9. Where Are You Now
10. Can't Make You Love Me
11. When Your Eyes Say It
12. Dear Diary

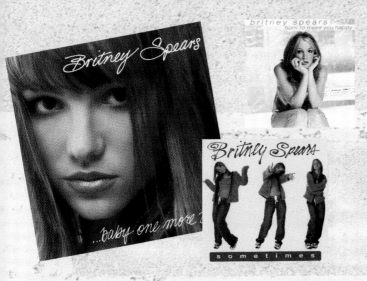

CD SINGLES

(in North America and/or Europe)

* **...Baby One More Time** (with dance remixes plus previously unreleased B-side "Autumn Goodbye")
* **Sometimes** (with dance remixes plus previously unreleased B-side "I'm So Curious")
* **Born To Make You Happy** (released only outside North America)
* **(You Drive Me) Crazy** (includes several remixes)
* **From The Bottom Of My Broken Heart** (radio edit plus additional remix of "Crazy")

Note: Several versions of many CD singles exist, with different "bonus tracks" depending on when and where the CD single was released.

HOME VIDEOS

If you're a big Brit fan, "Time Out With Britney Spears" (on VHS and DVD) is a must for your Britney collection. OK, the vid isn't going to win any Academy Awards for best documentary, but it's got plenty of stuff to keep you entertained for several viewings.

Britney starts the tape by giving a little background about her early days as a performer, when she was a budding gymnast instead of a singer! Eventually, of course, she went on to pursue a career in music, a career that got a huge lift from her role on Disney's "The New Mickey Mouse Club" in the mid-1990s.

Britney then takes you behind the scenes of the recording of her debut album in the spring of 1998 and for the filming of her first three music videos: "...Baby One More Time," "Sometimes" and "(You Drive Me) Crazy." While the backstage info is pretty interesting, perhaps the best part of this segment is the inclusion of all three music videos in their entirety. Since it's almost impossible to record a complete video off MTV these days (every vid on "TRL" is cut off way before it ends), you'll appreciate having Britney's videos in this collection.

Also featured are two performances from Britney's concert on The Disney Channel: "Born To Make You Happy" and "From The Bottom Of My Broken Heart."

One final bonus: Included with the video/DVD is a cassette sampler featuring new Jive Records artists such as Steps ("Tragedy") and Aaron Carter ("Girl You Shine"). The tunes are fun, so give 'em a listen.

BOOKS

Britney's new, official book, "Britney Spears' Heart to Heart," should be in stores by the time you read this. In the book, the American singing sensation and her mom talk about life, love, fame and following your dreams.

Britney makes success look simple. As Brit will tell you, though, success is hard work – you need talent, belief in yourself and someone else who believes in you. For Britney, that person has always been her mother, Lynne Spears, who is not just Britney's mom but also her best friend.

In "Britney Spears' Heart to Heart," Britney and Lynne share the inspiring story of how one little girl from Kentwood, La., turned into a music phenomenon. From the days of singing at talent shows and family gatherings to recording "...Baby One More Time" and performing with 'NSync, Britney and Lynne share intimate details about Britney's rise to stardom.

But this book is much more than just the story of Britney's life. In their own words, Lynne and Britney talk openly about the challenges facing all mothers and daughters. How do you encourage your child? How do you talk to your mom? How do you overcome obstacles? How do you talk about dating and relationships, dress codes, self-esteem and body image?

Featuring never-before-seen photos and dozens of behind-the-scenes stories about life at home, in the studio, and on the road, "Britney Spears' Heart to Heart" is not only a must-have for Britney fans, it's also an honest look at what it's like for girls to grow up in today's world.

THE BRITNEY DOLLS

Britney's three official dolls, which hit stores in time for the holidays, were a huge hit! Each doll came with separate outfits mirroring the clothes Britney wore in her first three music videos: "...Baby One More Time," "Sometimes" and "(You Drive Me) Crazy."

If you're an avid collector, buy all the dolls and keep them in their original boxes. They could be worth big money someday! ♥

Sightings!

Britney Spears

Britney Spears celebrates her 18th birthday with singer Robbie Carrico of Boyz N Girls United.

Britney flashes a smile at the premiere of "Drive Me Crazy," the movie for which Britney contributed the title song. TOP: The movie's star, Melissa Joan Hart, parties with Britney at the premiere. BOTTOM: Melissa (right) chats with Britney on MTV's "Total Request Live."

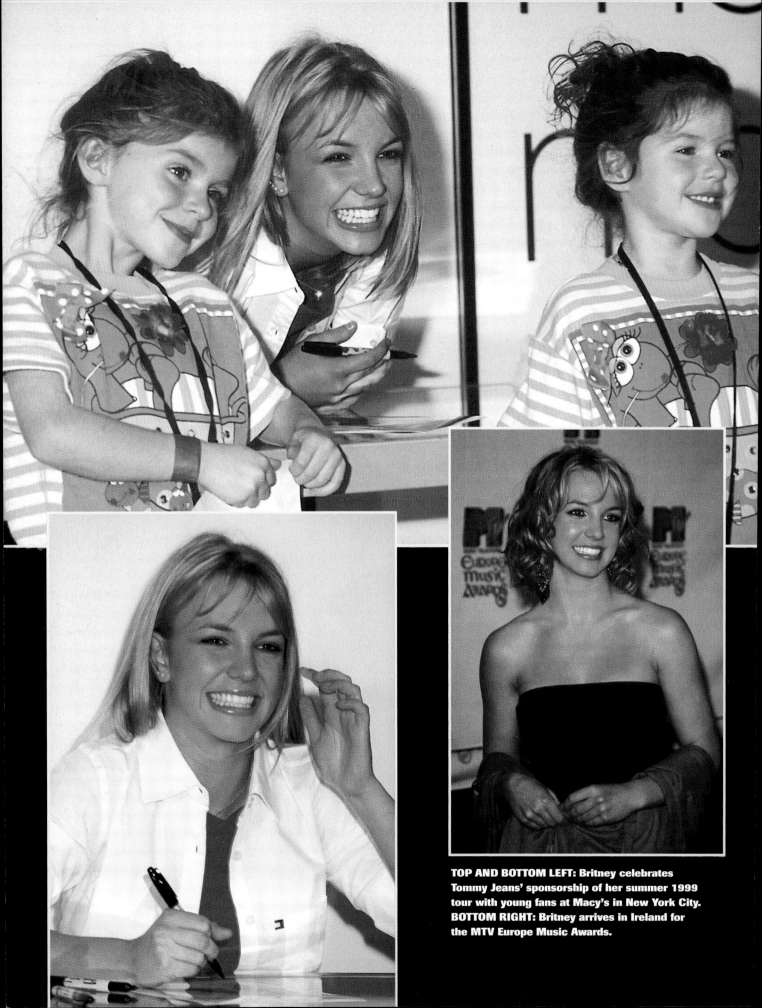

TOP AND BOTTOM LEFT: Britney celebrates Tommy Jeans' sponsorship of her summer 1999 tour with young fans at Macy's in New York City. **BOTTOM RIGHT:** Britney arrives in Ireland for the MTV Europe Music Awards.

Britney goes glamorous at the 2000 Grammy Awards, where she performed two songs and was nominated for Best New Artist.

Britney enjoys some rare time off to relax on a friend's boat.

MARK ALLAN/GLOBE (2)

Britney chats with MTV VJ Ananda
Lewis during a recent appearance
on "Total Request Live."

Britney hits the town with her mother Lynne at a pre-Grammy Awards party. BELOW: Britney hangs out with fellow Grammy nominee Marc Anthony.

BRITNEY ON THE GO!
TOP: At the MTV Europe Music Awards
BOTTOM: At the Billboard Music Awards
RIGHT: At a Teen People bash